The Lafaya Way®

Understanding Your Aspie Child

Lafaya Mitchell, LMFT

Co-Published by
Leverage Press/Hybrid Global Publishing
301 E 57th Street, 4th floor
New York, NY 10022

Copyright © 2019 by Lafaya Mitchell, LMFT

All rights reserved. No part of this book may be reproduced or transmitted in any form or by in any means, electronic or mechanical, including photocopying, recording, or by any information storage and retrieval system, without the written permission of the Publisher, except where permitted by law.

Manufactured in the United States of America, or in the United Kingdom when distributed elsewhere.

Author Lafaya Mitchell, LMFT

The Lafaya Way®

Understanding Your Aspie Child

ISBN: 978-1-948181-21-1

Cover Design by: Cynthia Lay
Interior Design: Leverage Press

Dedication

This book is dedicated to my absolutely wonderful husband and children. Thank you all for your endless love, support, and patience as I take the time away from you in my endeavor to change the world for the better, in the special way that I have been gifted to do so.

Acknowledgements

To Katherine McMahon for believing in me and forcing me to acknowledge there is something different and a little special about the way I do things. You helped materialize "The Lafaya Method" to light, assisting me to give birth to The Lafaya Way. Thank you from the bottom of my heart.

To Aunt Geraldine for helping me believe in my importance and giving me the courage to unapologetically be myself and share my gifts with the world.

To Auntie Renee for your nurturing ways that comfort me when I sulk and whine about not being able to do something.

To all the wise women who support me and give me the strength to press on. I love you all.

Table of Contents

Preface

Introduction

Chapter 1   1
Twelve Common Challenges and Difficult Traits in Aspie Children

Chapter 2   11
Common Effects of Aspie Symptomatology

Chapter 3   17
Trigger Point One
Communication Difficulties

Chapter 4   33
Trigger Point Two
Being Told "No"

Chapter 5   43
Trigger Point Three
Feeling Invalidated, Misunderstood or Judged

Chapter 6   **49**
Trigger Point Four
Aspies Treated as if They are
Lower Functioning

Chapter 7   **57**
Trigger Point Five
Sensory Issues

Chapter 8   **65**
Trigger Point Six
Struggles with Transitions/
Changes to Routine

Chapter 9   **73**
Trigger Point Seven
A New Way to View Hyper-Focus

Chapter 10   **89**
Conclusion

Preface

Welcome to the second book of
The Lafaya Way series,
Understanding Your Aspie Child.

The Lafaya Way series was written
to fill in the gaps that exist in proper
care for children with moderate to
severe social, emotional and
behavioral issues who may not
benefit from some of the other
more popular techniques such as
ABA (Applied Behavioral Analysis)
and DBT (Dialectical Behavioral
Therapy).

Most of the children that I work
with tend to experience similar

challenges (Aspie-like traits), especially hypersensitivity and strong reactivity to the sensory stimuli around them. In The Lafaya Way series, I specifically focus on their sensitivity to the internal states of others who are working with them.

In my first book, The Lafaya Way, A Fresh Approach to Parenting Hypersensitive Children, I outlined the philosophy I have developed throughout the decades of experience from working with difficult-to-treat populations. I specialize in Autism Spectrum Disorders, Reactive Attachment Disorders, and severe mood/anxiety disorders.

For those of you who have not read the first book, The Lafaya Way, A Fresh Approach to Parenting Hypersensitive Children, I highly recommend you do so because it provides the foundational advanced relational approach to parenting from which every book in the series is based.

This second book of The Lafaya Way series, Understanding Your Aspie Child is written to increase parental identification and understanding of Aspie traits while offering a fresh perspective on how to view and respond to those traits.

Introduction

I often use the term "Asp-hole" in this book when referring to Aspie-traits children. This is not to be offensive, but to emphasize the frustration caused by tough Aspie-like behavior and traits.

Your little Asp-hole may or may not have been diagnosed with Asperger's Syndrome or they may only appear to have some of the Asperger's symptomatology (Aspie Traits), without meeting the full criteria for a formal diagnosis of Asperger's.

The next few pages list questions for you to ask yourself to help you determine if this book is for you:

- Has your child been diagnosed with an Autism Spectrum Disorder (this includes Asperger's Syndrome)? **Y N**

- Has your child been diagnosed with **ADHD, ODD, RAD, ED** or any anxiety/mood, or other disorder, and you feel there is something more that is not being addressed or that the treatment of the diagnosed disorder is not working? **Y N**

- Have you done your research as a parent of a child who does not respond to treatment(s) and discovered that it seems a little (or a lot) like your child has Asperger's, but when you suggest this to the multiple practitioners whom your child has seen, they shoot down the idea because your child can sometimes manage eye contact and for the most part is able to participate in reciprocal conversations?

Y N

- Does your child suffer from extreme sensitivity and unusual reactivity to situations that do not elicit such reactivity in others?

Y N

- Are you, your child's school or daycare staff, and other caregivers at a loss of what to do with your unruly, out of control child?

Y N

- Is your child currently undiagnosed, however, manifesting concerning behaviors which are disrupting appropriate social functioning (irking you and everyone else with their over-the-top behaviors)?   Y   N

If you answered yes to one or more of these questions, this book is for you!

The purpose of The Lafaya Way series is to offer hope through a new way of relating to the hypersensitive, difficult-to-manage child.

The Lafaya Way, Understanding Your Aspie Child, was written to enhance your understanding of what your child is experiencing so you may learn to empathize with them, to more effectively respond to and teach your difficult child.

Chapter 1

Twelve Common Challenges and Difficult Traits in Aspie Children

"It is impossible to effectively deal with a matter, without first understanding it."

-Lafaya Mitchell

Children with Aspie traits have areas of challenge, which tend to impede their ability to function in socially acceptable ways. If you are looking to create manageable interactions with your child, it is important to recognize and understand the symptomatology associated with the struggles of Aspie children.

Some of the symptoms or traits of the Aspie child that can cause the most disruption are outlined on the following pages:

1. Extreme Impulsivity

The Aspie child goes from 0 to 60 in their reactions. In part, this extreme reactivity stems from the fact that "the novelty does not often wear off," when they are upset or traumatized by an event. For example, if there is a current event happening that is similar to a past upsetting event, the Aspie child reacts as if he/she is reliving the most explosive part of the past event. The 0 to 60 in their reaction can also come from a sense of hopelessness in things not getting better and feeling they lack control over themselves or their given circumstances.

2. Tunnel Vision

Aspies often only see or focus on their area(s) of interest. Often, there is one specific area of hyper-focus, in which they constantly obsess.

3. Black and White Thinking

They take what is said by others literally and often have a difficult time understanding jokes or ironic statements.

4. Struggles with Abstract Thought Processes

The Aspie has trouble with looking at things removed from the fact of the here-and-now. In other words, telling them if they do not finish their vegetables, they will not grow up to be big and strong will not convince them to eat their veggies.

To the Aspie, what they are doing now has nothing to do with a future they can't see.

5. Sensitivities to Sensory Input

Sensitivity to sensory input (taste, touch, smell, sight, and/or hearing) may seem odd or excessive (i.e., a child reacting to the sound of a motorcycle with surprising panic-like responses, including jumping, tensing, screaming).

6. Food Sensitivities

Food Sensitivities are quite common among Aspies who are often referred to as finicky eaters. (This critically relevant area will be discussed in detail in Chapter 7).

7. EF Challenges

Executive function (EF) is a set of processes, related to managing oneself and one's resources in order to achieve a goal. Executive function struggles contribute to challenges with starting and/or completing projects, organizing tasks, etc.

8. Attention & Focus Difficulties

Attention and/or focus are especially problematic when you try to have Aspies focus on a subject other than their area of hyper-focus.

They may also struggle when they don't see the logic in being asked to do something, especially if they feel that a task is pointless or mundane.

It is senseless for Aspies to do things like repetitive math calculations or cleaning their bedroom that will become messy again.

9. Difficulties Showing or Recognizing Social Cues

Many Aspies do not show much emotion, unless they are angry. It is difficult to know if an Aspie child is enjoying something due to lack of facial expressions. Conversely, Aspies do not read cues from others very well, which often causes a great deal of awkwardness during social interactions.

10. Trouble with Transitions

Trouble with transitions includes adverse reactions when transitioning from one place to another, from one activity to another, and general changes in structure and routine.

11. Lack of Physical Coordination

This can be frustrating to parents who feel their child should have outgrown being so clumsy by a certain age.

12. There Are Quite A Few Symptoms That I Did Not List Here

I highly recommend that you search on YouTube for a segment entitled, "My Autism," by George. He gives a fantastic glimpse into the world of a child on the autism spectrum.

When I viewed the video, it made me cry because it contains the material I have been explaining to parents with children on the Spectrum or with Spectrum traits.

Chapter 2

Common Effects of Aspie Symptomatology

"The harder the conflict, the more glorious the triumph."

-Thomas Paine

Extensive damage is often done to the self-concept of children with difficult-to-manage Social, Emotional, and/or Behavioral (SEB) issues and children with ASD often fall into this category. SEB children are often confused and upset by the mere fact that they just can't "get it right." These children are often their own worst critics, continuously engaging in negative self-talk. They often repeat the negative things they hear and/or "feel" coming from others. Their self-esteem is often crushed and they cover-up their fear and sadness with anger and frustration and find themselves unable to change even when they hate how much they are disliked by others.

With this in mind, you may be asking yourself, "Why do Asp-holes seem to get a kick out of annoying the crap out of others when not being liked by others makes them feel bad?" One of my educated guesses is that over the years, the combination of social awkwardness, miscommunication, difficulty reading and responding appropriately to social cues, and other challenges leaves these children feeling like they annoy others anyway. It ultimately becomes easier and seemingly more satisfying to the wounded ego to be annoying on purpose as opposed to being annoying without truly intending to be. I've had many Aspies express that they are constantly frustrated by other people's judgments, illogical thinking, exaggerated emotions and unsolicited opinions and are just fighting back with their personal brand of irritation.

We can also take into account the possible impact of the lack of mirror neurons which aids in the ability to connect to and imitate the actions of others, which in turn makes it difficult for them to be affected by the reactions of others.

After identifying some of the symptomatology and resulting challenges, it is important to mention here that one of the things that makes most Aspies tough to deal with, even more so than your lower functioning ASD child, is they often resemble what I call "passers." My definition of a "passer" is someone who appears mostly "normal" so the behavior that comes from their symptomatology does not necessarily look disordered. However, the behavior looks more like defiance, non-compliance, or like they just simply don't care. This often results in them continually being punished or disliked, which lowers their self-esteem, and heightens their self-hatred, leading to the constant questioning of why they were made this way. There are many things, some mentioned above, effecting their ability to show the awesome child that they truly are. As parents, our obligation is to support our children to become the best <u>they</u> can be.

Chapter 3

Trigger Point One

Communication Difficulties

"The biggest communication problem is we do not listen to understand. We listen to reply."

-Wallace Huey & Peter Shepherd

In order to better assist you with learning how to more effectively raise your little Asp-hole, you need to have a clear understanding of their common triggers. Although you may already identify most of your child's triggers, some triggers may come as a surprise to you or have simply gone unacknowledged.

Expressive & Receptive Communication Difficulties

Communication difficulties is one of the most challenging issues when interacting with an Aspie. Language processing issues (both **receptive,** what's being said to them and **expressive,** what they are trying to say) present barriers to effective communication.

Do you ever get the feeling that an Aspie child does not understand the words coming out of your mouth when you are trying to talk to him/her? Even if the Aspie child is highly intelligent, he/she may have difficulties communicating and comprehending.

Psychological testing for children on both the low and high end of the autism spectrum often identifies some form and varying degrees of language processing issues.

This can be exacerbated by tough exchanges in which emotions may be so high that the anxiety of the situation triggers a sensory overload.

This either causes a "shut down" and the brain stops trying to process what is being communicated or the other end of the continuum which causes the "blow up" effect in which all the gaskets are smoking and the "Houston, we have a problem" dynamic occurs and an explosion is soon to follow.

Avoiding Potential Potholes (APPs)

Keep in mind that the "novelty does not wear off" issue (explained in Chapter 1) may play a significant part in the child's tough reactions during communication exchanges.

This is crucial to identify if you are dealing with a receptive or expressive communication issue.

Now let's take a deeper look at how receptive and expressive language processing affect communication.

Expressive Communication

Once, I worked with a teenager who shared that trying to express himself, especially when upset, is comparable to trying to fit an entire dictionary onto one page of paper. He expressed it was just easier to walk away and become avoidant than to try to release all that was going on in his brain out of his mouth.

This child was highly intelligent, and in this circumstance, his high intelligence coincides with an active brain (many thoughts at the same time). Therefore, his brain was working against him as he tried to communicate.

Can you imagine the frustration of knowing you should be smart enough to have something to say, and can't figure out how to release it properly? I have met many highly intelligent children who reach the conclusion that they must not be as intelligent as they thought. Worse yet, they feel they suffer from some serious deficiency, leaving them with the inability to express themselves, further damaging their "good-old" self-esteem.

Receptive Communication

Receptive language processing might also be impacted by an over-active brain and/or concrete thinking. You may find that sometimes when you are trying to joke around with an Aspie, the child simply does not get it, especially during intense interactions where a person is attempting to lighten the situation by joking. Often, this feels incongruent and condescending to an Aspie, especially if he/she is a black and white thinker.

Hyper-focus in restricted areas of interest may also disrupt receptive language processing. Aspies often tune out anything that is not related to their areas of interest. Emotional reactivity also strongly impacts language processing.

I will address hyper-focus more in Chapter 9.

Tips for Reducing Emotional Reactivity in Your Child:

1. Reduce your own emotional reactivity; this may be the single most important element to reducing strong reactivity in your Aspie Child. For more information on how to reduce emotional reactivity, see the "Core 4" of The Lafaya Way in the first book of the series.

2. Verbalize and validate what may

be triggering your child's responses during difficult moments. I recommend you use the list in Chapter 1: Twelve Common Challenges and Difficult Traits in Aspie Children as a reference to what may be occurring with your child).

Bringing awareness to what may be impacting the child helps them to gain logical perspective which reduces the intensity of emotions.

Language to Use:

1. When the "Novelty Doesn't Wear Off"

"You seem to be upset about (name the request) that I thought I made nicely. Are you still upset from what happened last time when I asked you to (name the request), when I was in a bad mood and we ended up in a big argument? Please remember, we're both working on saying things better, that's why I tried to say/ask in a calm way this time. Is there another way that I can say it so you feel better?"

*If needed, you can add:

"I know that we've had a hard time in this area before, however, I'm going to do my part to try to make things easier and to have you feel better about how we're relating to each other."

Please keep in mind that "less is more" when it comes to words, so only use the additional words if the child continues to argue.

Let me just toss in, that I know you may have a little Asp-hole that might give you a negative response the first time by possibly saying:

"You can just not say it to me at all."

If there has been a lot of friction in the area that you are addressing, expect that the little Asp-hole will have their comebacks. Try not to personalize their behavior. If you do, it creates more anxiety. Aspies are not fond of change (whether positive or negative). The important thing is to stay consistent with the message, "everyone wants peace in your home."

In case you're wondering, trying the

"let's have peace" approach two or three times does not make it a consistent effort. If it's been a tough interaction for an extended period, expect that it will take some time (even weeks or months) to provoke new responses. Remember for the Aspie, the novelty does not easily wear off.

2. Black and White Thinking

"Sometimes you tend towards concrete, black and white thinking. Did you take what I said literally because it was not my goal to upset you. What did you experience me saying?"

3. Not Interesting to You

"I know that what I'm talking about is not very interesting to you.

However, it's important that you hear me because I don't want you to feel like you are in trouble when I have to react to you not listening to me."

"The point I was trying to make was _____. Did you get something else from what I said? How can I say it better to make the point I was trying to make?"

4. Difficulty Expressing Themselves

"You seem to be having a difficult time expressing what you need" or "do you need some additional time to process it all and come back to me?"

"What you are saying right now is not the best way to say it to get your needs met, likely because you're really upset. Did you mean to say, _____?"

"Try saying it in another way so that I can hear you and you can feel heard/listened to, because the way you're saying it now can only serve to get you into trouble and I know that's not your real intention."

"Do you want to come back later, after you have had a chance to think about what you need?"

There are various ways to address breakdowns in communication.

The most important thing to do is to identify the contributing factors. The rest becomes easier as you master reacting to the facts as opposed to your emotions surrounding your interactions.

Chapter 4

Trigger Point Two
Being Told No

"Strong-willed children often grow into strong-willed adults who become world leaders, world shapers, and world changers. Parenting them peacefully is not only possible, it's imperative because sowing peace in their hearts now while they're in our care will grow a future of peace later when the world is in their care."

-L.R. Knost

Have you noticed the Aspie child is almost allergic to being told "No?" Over the years, many parents have expressed their frustrations. I am consistently hearing, "They just can't handle being told no."

Let me explain the logic I have discovered regarding this all too common problem when dealing with Asp-holes. As I mentioned before, Aspies tend to be very concrete thinkers, so when they are told no, to them it means "no" forever. This is why you often get the response as if "it's the end of the world" when you tell them no, because to them it almost is.

It can be tricky to find a good balance when telling "No" to a child who is an "instant gratification-requiring child." Every individual in this world is told "no" so it is unrealistic to teach your child otherwise.

Remember, being told no is upsetting to the Aspie child for reasons unique to them. The more you understand and empathize with the child's sensitivity to being told "no," the better you will respond, which increases the likelihood that the Aspie child will be more accepting when told "no."

I repeatedly suggest for parents to avoid the overall "no" to try to lessen the high reactivity you often receive from most Aspie children.

I have learned that it is more effective to soften your "no" a bit with creative verbalizing. This is done with the understanding that their concrete brains think no means no*forever.*

Example(s)

"Not right now, but you can definitely do/have (desired activity/item) after (waiting for a better time/doing required task)."

Avoiding Potential Potholes (APPs)

Often, Aspie children continue to insist they get what they want immediately. When you run into these situations, it is helpful to clarify that he/she will likely miss out on what they want when they are too pushy.

Remind them not to sabotage themselves.

If it has to be a "no" indefinitely for reasons that are not in your control, use the following language:

"I wish I could, however, I am not able to do (request of child) right now. I'd be happy to (more plausible alternative)."

Again, the child may pursue "getting what they want." It can be helpful to validate their experience with language such as:

"I know that you hate being told no and I am trying to get you (more plausible alternative) instead of nothing. Please don't keep yourself from getting at least (more plausible alternative)."

The strong-willed Aspie may still endure. If so, establish your boundaries and stick to them without a lot of extra discussion or emotion. If they earn nothing by persisting, then so be it.

Please refrain from judging them for

earning nothing; it is what it is. (For more on letting go and letting consequences remain, refer back to the first book of The Lafaya Way series).

In situations where the answer will always be no because what your child is asking for is bad for their health and/or well-being, use the following language:

> "I know that you really want (the unsafe thing). The truth is (the unsafe thing) is bad for you. It's my job to keep you safe even if you don't like me sometimes when I do."

Please note that the effectiveness of these types of interactions increase over time and improves exponentially with your ability as a parent to keep your internal cool and remain non-judgmental.

Keep in mind your internal experience when saying "no" has to be managed as well. For many parents, it can be upsetting to feel they are "unable" to give their child what they want because the child has not earned it, has been misbehaving, or the parent simply doesn't have the budget for it.

Be careful to manage your feelings of guilt when unable to give the child what they want, especially if you feel as if your parents did not meet your wants when you were a child. If you have thoughts like, "if you would just do "X" then I would not have to keep things from you," this may increase your feelings of resentment towards your child, which keeps you from being a more effective parent.

Potholes of Personalization (PoPs)

Think of being personally offended by your child's misbehavior as a pothole to be avoided.

Steering away from PoPs prevents avoidable damage and reduces unnecessary repairs to maintain functionality in relationships. If you continuously disregard these types of potholes, you risk causing irreparable damage to your relationship.

For a better understanding of how to reduce personalization, refer to Chapter 6 in the first book of The Lafaya Way series.

Avoiding Potential Potholes (APPs)

If there have been times in the past where the child has been told "no" in a similar circumstance and there has been an emotionally charged outcome, it will take a while to get the Aspie child past the "novelty doesn't wear off" phenomena.

For the full explanation, see Chapter 7 in the first book, of The Lafaya Way series.

Chapter 5

Trigger Point Three

Feeling Invalidated, Misunderstood or Judged

"Being misunderstood by someone is vexation. Being misunderstood by everyone is tragedy."

-Liu Shahe

Feeling misunderstood, judged, and uncared for are the primary complaints leading to the highest levels of reactivity from the numerous Aspie children I have worked with throughout the years.

First, I need to reiterate, "your Aspie child is a little (or a lot) different from your neurotypical child" (you can look at it however you want to, but some difference needs to be acknowledged). Their brains function differently, they understand differently, they have interests that often seem a bit strange or excessive when compared to their peers, and their emotional reactivity can be much stronger for various reasons.

Often, they have failed miserably for years at trying to interact with other human beings, which is why they often prefer to be alone or with animals.

Now some parents may accept that their child is a little different, which there is **NOTHING** wrong with; yet expect their child to respond as a neurotypical child would. These parents become upset when their Aspie child does not respond "rightfully."

A call to action for parents of Aspie children is to consider that "right" reactions for one child is not necessarily "right" for another child.

> **"If you do not accept your child for who he/she is, and do not establish a judgment-free zone, you will continue to have difficult interactions with your child."**

Establishing a judgment-free zone requires some bridge-building efforts to achieve more "appropriate" behaviors and responses from your child.

One example of bridge building is, if you expect your Aspie child to validate others, demonstrate greater understanding and reduce judgment towards others, you as the parent have to model those behaviors towards them first.

Chapter 6

Trigger Point Four

Aspies Being Treated as if They are Lower Functioning

"Inclusion is not a strategy to help people fit into the systems and structures which exist in our societies; it is about transforming those systems and structures to make it better for everyone."

-Diane Richler

Trigger point four speaks for itself. There is often an issue with the Aspie child being treated as if they're lower functioning than they actually are.

One common parental mistake is to treat the Aspie child as the younger sibling even when he/she is chronologically older.

The neurotypical younger sibling often becomes "parentified." Parentification is the process of a role reversal whereby a younger neurotypical child is obliged to act as a parental figure and treats the older Aspie sibling as if they were under their care.

Parents tend to have higher

expectations of the younger neurotypical child and require him/her to look out for their older Aspie sibling.

This crushes the Aspie's self-esteem and induces high reactivity from the older Aspie child who understands that the younger sibling is being treated as if he/she is more responsible and "better" functioning.

I know it can be tough navigating a situation in which it appears the younger neurotypical sibling has a greater capacity to handle things in life in a more mature way than their older Aspie sibling. It's important to gain an understanding of how to support your older Aspie child to take on his/her role as the older sibling in the household, which will build confidence and self-esteem, encouraging more mature behavior.

If your household has a younger sibling constantly telling the older sibling what to do, tattling whenever they feel the older sibling did something wrong, then such dynamics need to change.

First, start emphasizing your role as the parent and let the younger sibling know that it is not their job to tell the older sibling what to do: it's yours.

Next, clarify with the older sibling that they are older.

Tell them that you know it has been a mistake over the years to let the younger sibling act as if they were the oldest and now you are going to work to correct that error. This will facilitate the healing process for your bruised Aspie child.

There may also be some healing necessary related to the mishandling of Aspie children within the school system, which often damages their self-esteem. It is common for the Aspie child to either not be allowed any accommodations because their IQ (intelligence) is too high, or to receive inappropriate accommodations, which either places them in special education classrooms for lower functioning children or with IEP/504 plans that do not properly address their needs.

Parents, please pay close attention to the statement below:

> *"It is imperative that you do your due diligence. Examine the classrooms, groups, programs, etc. that the professionals try to place your Aspie child in."*

Thoroughly review the programs (i.e. therapy groups, classroom environments, day camps, etc.) before sending your Aspie child to make sure that it is a good fit.

I cannot tell you how many children have had their self-esteem crushed by being placed in a setting with low functioning children. Aspie children are concrete thinkers, so they start to question whether or not they are as low functioning as the children they see around them and just don't know it or worse, believe that this may be how people view them.

Placing Aspies in the wrong programs also breeds a mistrust of adults and other authority figures, contributing to difficulties complying with what people tell them is best for them.

Ultimately, placing Aspies in lower functioning roles and situations chips away at their self-esteem, which tends to lead to more Aspholish behavior.

Chapter 7

Trigger Point Five

Sensory Issues

"There is only one way to look at things until someone shows us how to look at them with different eyes."

-Pablo Picasso

The sensory issue triggers are often missed. Sensory issues range from mild to extremely severe. The impact of sensory dysregulation (impairment in the regulation of a physiological and/or psychological process) can be subtle and sometimes delayed. There are a wide variety of sensory issues experienced by the sensitive child. The sensory dysregulation can manifest by having moderate to extreme sensitivities to sounds, tastes, textures, smells, sights, and touch. Because there is significant variance in the type and intensity of the sensitivities, the sensory issues sometimes go unidentified.

Food Sensitivities

Children can be sensitive to the flavor, texture, smell or even the sight of certain foods. They may even be put off by how long it takes to chew certain foods. The intensity of these sensitivities can be extremely high for Aspie children. Just imagine nails on a chalkboard or someone pouring an entire box of salt into your bowl of food. I know this example seems overly dramatic, however, it helps envision what Aspies often experience when overwhelmed with sensory input.

Be careful not to accuse them of over-exaggerating simply because you cannot relate to their heightened sensitivity.

Their experience with sensory input is often not the same as your experience with similar sensory input. For example, if an Aspie child gags every time they try a crunchy vegetable, he/she may not be over-exaggerating and may have sensitivity to the texture of crunchy vegetables.

Variation in sensitivities leads parents to often label their Aspie child as a finicky eater. To make matters worse, the extremeness of sensitivities and the difficulty getting over a negative or traumatic experience with certain stimuli, including an experience with food can cause them to dislike a food they once preferred on their slim list of food choices.

Food issues are common and often frustrating to both the child and parents. Sensory issues can also be tactile; the annoying brush of the tags on their clothes, a light touch on the arm, or the feeling of long sleeve shirts, pants, or socks. Sensory issues can also come in the form of sounds that are sudden, too loud, too quiet, and even annoying like the hum of an air conditioner. Whatever the sensory issue, it can cause a sudden agitation in the Aspie child, exhibiting negative reaction immediately or after some time. The child may be having a meltdown due to a negative sensory experience and nobody can figure out what triggered it, not even the child.

In situations where there doesn't seem to be any real provocation that you can see for your sensitive child's upset, you may want to utilize the H.A.L.T. check-in method created long ago. It's a simple check to see if they are Hungry, Angry, Lonely, and/or Tired that can help identify potential reasons for the negative reactions. I like to use the H.A.L.T.S. method for children with sensory issues. The S stands for sensory overload. It can be helpful to cognitively identify the reason for an extreme and/or seemingly unprovoked, emotional response. (The original H.A.L.T. method is borrowed from 12-Step Programs and I have modified it by adding the "S" for sensory overload).

Chapter 8

Trigger Point Six

Struggles with Transitions or Changes to Routine

"Life is like a rollercoaster, it goes up, down, and all around."

-Morgan Washington

Struggles with transitions and changes to routine are common complaints for parents of children with Aspie traits. It is often upsetting to parents to experience marked difficulty with preparing their child to get ready for school, to go to bed on time, return to school after a break, go from the house into the car, go to new places, having visitors over, etc.

The struggles with transitions and changes in routine are largely due to the fact that Aspie children tend not to have the flexibility to move from one area of focus to another. Let's face it, sometimes it feels as if they are moving like turtles unless they are going to a preferred activity.

The inherent tendency for the Aspie to lag behind is often met by extreme frustration from most parents who prefer punctuality. This disrupts any internal peace the parent may have had before venturing to coax their reluctant child to move at a faster pace.

The combination of the child's frustration with being "forced" into the uncomfortable situation of transitioning from one activity to another and the parent's frustration with being held hostage by their slow-moving child, often results in strained interactions.

Some Tips for Combatting the Transition Struggle Blues

1. Be Pro-Active

Try to prepare your child ahead of time for how things will be sequenced that day so they are not surprised by a seemingly out of nowhere prompt to transition (the more detail you provide the better).

2. Establish a Standard Routine

Consistency in routines and structure often eases the Aspie's mind.

3. Set the Transition Times Earlier Than You Want with Your Child

If you need to be out of the door by

9:00 a. m., tell the child you need to be out of the door by 8:30 a. m. or earlier if they are especially turtle-like. This way, by the time you are vocalizing the urgency of needing to get out by 8:30, your emotions will know that you still have 30 minutes and your already anxious emotion-soaking child will not draw from your strong internal anxiety. (For more information on emotion-soaking, refer to the first book in The Lafaya Way series).

A Few Tips for Easing Routine Disruption

1. Start "Practicing" for the New Routine Ahead of Time

For example, if a child is returning to school after

summer break, start to move their bedtimes up incrementally over the break. Please remember to be proactive in this process by letting your child know ahead of time that you will do this to help them adapt slowly to avoid sudden changes.

2. Expect Struggles with Routine

Emphasize that changes in routine can be difficult, and be prepared for any bad feelings. This way, the Aspie child is ready for battle by using their coping skills.

3. Find Ways to Heavily Reinforce

To reward positive responses to changes in routine, use effective reinforcements for your child, (i.e. extra 15 minutes of gaming time, favorite snack, verbal praise, etc.).

Trigger Point Six: Struggles with Transitions/Changes to Routine

Make it a big deal that they combated the tendency to get upset with changes in routine.

Chapter 9

Trigger Point Seven

A New Way to View Hyper-Focus

"Often we look so long at the closed door that we do not see the one that has been opened for us."

-Helen Keller

One area that can truly make an Aspie seem really "Asp-holish" is hyper-focus in restricted areas of interest. Sometimes or maybe almost all of the time, it can feel nearly impossible to tear them away from either discussing and/or engaging in activities associated with their restricted area(s) of interest.

There is a great deal of variation in specific areas of hyper-focus for Aspies. No matter what the area of interest, it can hinder daily functioning depending on the severity. I'm sure many of you can relate to the experience of trying to encourage, coax, or otherwise gain compliance from your child in doing tasks outside of their area(s) of interest and feeling as if you are failing miserably in your attempts.

Often, trying to pull them away from what they want to do results in arguing, meltdown behavior, and/or just plain old defiance by ignoring your request. The daily or near daily occurrence of these types of altercations creates great strains in the family dynamics if not handled correctly. The goal of this section is to assist you to gain a more productive perspective in the area of hyper-focus, and to help you deal in a more positive, self-esteem building, and effective way with areas of hyper-focus.

Although hyper-focus on restricted

areas of interest can be exhausting to deal with at times, there are also some positives to it.

I'll warn you ahead of time that you may not like this section much because I am going to describe some of the positives for hyper-focus.

I am sharing this in the hopes that it will open your mind and heart to the opportunity to use the positive aspects of hyper-focus to build up your child's self-esteem and to reduce your own irritation and frustration about their hyper-focus. This improves your ability to have better interactions with your child through the reduction of negative emotions being transmitted in their direction, which reduces defensiveness and stubborn refusal to do what you ask.

It takes hyper-focus in only one area to develop the most inventive genius (imagine Albert Einstein). Most, if not all of the advancements in technology that we have had has been the result of single-minded focus.

Many historical geniuses were outcasts, often shunned by society for their complete focus on their area of interest and the inability to interact in basic social situations. It's important to find the value of hyper-focus if we are to assist our children to acknowledge the importance of interacting with others.

Companies like Google actively search for and hire individuals on the spectrum because they know that new inventions often stem from the genius created from a focused effort in one area of interest.

One of the most valuable weapons at your disposal is your ability to connect to and appreciate the strengths of another person whom you are trying to influence. Valuing their interests is especially important for raising self-esteem in Aspies.

When you can relate to their

experience of what is important to them as opposed to judging it negatively, you gain their willingness to be interested in what you have to say because you are speaking their language.

Keep in mind that there are both good and bad aspects to hyper-focus. The trick is to learn how to focus on the positive when you speak to the Aspie. A helpful statement may be, "It is really good that you have so much skill and interest in ____, however, balancing what we like to do with cooperating to meet each other's needs is necessary for a happy life."

As a protective parent, you can speak to a desire to make sure that hyper-focus does not become a point of obsession that puts the Aspie in situations where they are getting in trouble at home or school. It may become necessary to put very strict limitations or not have certain things around at all if it's going to hurt them to pull themselves away from it.

Finding the positives, reinforcing that there is genius afoot, and addressing Aspies in a validating way when it is time to move away from the activity can significantly reduce the tension surrounding areas of hyper-focus.

When you learn to embrace the positive attributes regarding their area of interest, it strengthens their self-esteem. Stronger self-esteem leads to greater success relating to others because it decreases that inner feeling of being unlovable and no good.

Please don't get me wrong, I am not suggesting that you should not work towards balance where it's necessary. What I am saying is that,

it's just an area worth identifying; as to whether or not there is a way to strengthen the way you relate to your child.

To sum it up, locate the positive and encourage the genius connected to hyper-focus while helping your child balance out what they like with what is required to be a productive member of your household and society.

Validate the experience of the single-minded focus while teaching them to navigate their social world in a way that will create a sense of connection with others for them to be happy.

The real goal as parents is not to have children behave in the ways that we think are "right" for us per se, however, that they behave in

Trigger Point Seven: A New Way to View Hyper-Focus

ways that will promote a happy, healthy, well-functioning existence for them. When we make it our jobs to decide how they are to behave based on our limited experience of how people should behave, we prevent our children from being "free" to be the best person they can be.

Again, I am not suggesting that you allow your child to breech yours or others' boundaries or to do harm to themselves or others through their activities. Please, take a step back and evaluate your reasoning when you have a difficult time with something your child is focused on.

If they are not doing harm to themselves or others, the consistent emphasis and understanding that everyone in the home needs to do their part to keep an orderly household should be your only focus.

It's especially important to take self-inventory when it seems like you are judging your Aspie child and wishing they could be more like you or someone else.

Now, minus the judgment and the thinking that they should "want" to do their part will cause you to be more persuasive than you have been previously.

The keys to finding balance are:

1. Check Yourself First

Are you coming from a place of judgment and expecting/ desiring that your child react or function differently when addressing the area of hyper- focus? If so, work to move out of that stance as it will only make them feel like you don't appreciate them for who they are and want them to be someone they're not.

2. Ask Yourself: Are They Doing Harm to Themselves or Others?

Understanding there is no "true" harm (threat to safety and/ or health) from the area of hyper-focus, can help reduce over-reactivity and increase focus on problem-solving.

3. Think of Ways for Your Aspie Child to Connect

If, for the sake of fairness you are asking each member in the family to do their part, ***emphasize*** that everyone is to do their part. Steer away from expressing that if the Aspie cared more about you, they'd want to contribute more.

The Aspie's resistance to participate has little to do with their personal feelings about you. However, if you are irritating them by saying "they don't care," this will eventually cause them not to care. In addition, if they feel like your complaints have more to do with the fact that they don't derive the same satisfaction that you do from doing things for others, this too will make them less likely to cooperate. Remember they have their own areas of interest that occupies much of their brain energy.

Be creative when combating areas of hyper-focus. Keep in mind that it is an area, which often consumes the Aspie's thoughts.

This is extremely difficult, even emotionally, for them to tear themselves away from their area(s) of interest.

Try to find a comparison of something or someone that you have a hard time tearing yourself away from, how much you miss it or miss them when they are away and empathize with their experience as opposed to judging it. It also helps to find the positives with them having an area of hyper-focus, as it will give you the tools you need to build their self-esteem, validate their experience and soften the blow of them needing to step away from the activity to address other functional areas of need for the allotted time necessary.

Chapter 10
Conclusion

"The only disability in life is a bad attitude."

-Scott Hamilton

The primary purpose of writing "The Lafaya Way, Understanding Your Aspie Child" is to increase your understanding of the many challenges that Aspie children experience and promote an informed and positive handling of such hypersensitive children.

Trigger points such as: communication difficulties (including struggles with expressive/receptive language processing), feeling misunderstood, being treated as if they are lower functioning, and sensory issues, are some of the areas contributing to many of the predominant Asp-hole tendencies.

Conclusion

The Lafaya Way, Understanding Your Aspie Child also identifies a new way to view areas of hyper-focus and use them as powerful self-esteem building tools that can fully support your Aspie child gain recognition amongst our next generation of geniuses!

It is most imperative to learn to hold closely the importance of your continued self-awareness and self-improvement work in order to reduce the personalization of your Asp-hole's difficult behaviors (remember PoPs).

My purpose for writing the "The Lafaya Way" series is for parents of difficult hypersensitive children to one day say, "With help from The Lafaya Way, my child is not such a little Asphole after all!"

I would love to hear how this advanced relational approach has impacted you and your family's life. Please drop me a note.

Lafaya@pomtsolutions.com

If you would like more education, strategies and techniques to support you in dealing with the behavioral difficulties of your Aspie-trait child, please visit:

www.pomtsolutions.com/media

YouTube@lafayaway.com

To contact Lafaya Mitchell, LMFT for speaking engagements, parent education classes, family sessions, and more, please visit:

www.pomtsolutions.com/contact

www.ingramcontent.com/pod-product-compliance
Lightning Source LLC
Chambersburg PA
CBHW071743080526
44588CB00013B/2134